PALEOZOIC ERA

CAMBRIAN PERIOD	ORDOVICIAN PERIOD	SILURIAN PERIOD	DEVONIAN PERIOD	CARBONIFEROUS PERIOD	PERMIAN PERIOD
544–505 million years ago	505–438 million years ago	438–410 million years ago	410–360 million years ago	360–286 million years ago	286–248 million years ago

IN THE PAST

David Elliott

illustrated by
Matthew Trueman

CANDLEWICK PRESS

MESOZOIC ERA			CENOZOIC ERA		
TRIASSIC PERIOD	**JURASSIC PERIOD**	**CRETACEOUS PERIOD**	**PALEOGENE PERIOD**	**NEOGENE PERIOD**	**QUATERNARY PERIOD**
248–208 million years ago	208–144 million years ago	144–65 million years ago	65–24 million years ago	24–1.8 million years ago	1.8 million years ago–present

CAMBRIAN PERIOD

544–505 million years ago

Trilobite

So many of you.
So long ago.
So much above you.
Little below.
Now you lie hidden
deep in a clock,
uncountable ticks
silenced by rock.

ORDOVICIAN PERIOD

505 – 438 million years ago

Astraspis

No jaws.
No fins.
Only six inches long.
One note at the beginning
Of a never-ending song.

Eurypterus

Curious?
Bored?
Or desperate for the warm sun
on your armored back?

Some say you were among
the first to leave the ocean
and touch the wet black
earth.

We're glad you did,
for what it's worth.

Dunkleosteus

You weren't picky
when it came to diet;
if it lived in the ocean,
you would try it,
which leads me to raise
this delicate question:

Your face—
the unhappy result
of indigestion?

Meganeura

No birds yet.
Only you in the sky.
Meganeuropsis permiana:
the giant dragonfly!

Arthropleura

The bad news: Like a centipede. Eight feet long. Or more.
The good news: *Arthropleura* was an herbivore.

Dimetrodon

You might have been a carnivore,
but you were *not* a dinosaur.
(You and yours
came long before.)
Factual,
but I've a hunch
it made no difference
to your lunch.

Eoraptor

One
of
the
great-
grand-
fathers.
One
of
Nature's
little
jokes.
One
of those
acorns
that
produces
mighty
oaks.

Dilophosaurus

Blessed
with
crests!

Stegosaurus

Your brain?
The size
of a
walnut.
Your bulk?
Immense.
Which proves
there's some-
thing more
to life
than just
intelligence.

Apatosaurus

They changed your name
from *thunder*—
from thunder to *deceptive*.

Some liked it.
Some were not receptive.

Whatever name they call you,
it's only nomenclature.
No single word describes you,
Great Wonderment of Nature!

Brachytrachelopan

Your neck too short!
Your tail too long!
Somehow you're
put together wrong.
And that name!
You should renounce it.
It takes a genius
to pronounce it.

JURASSIC PERIOD

208 – 144 million years ago

Yutyrannus

Your discovery in China
created quite a stir.
Could dinosaurs be feathered?
They could. You were.
The proof is in the rocks,
those impressions that surround you.
I imagine they were tickled
the moment that they found you.

CRETACEOUS PERIOD
144–65 million years ago

Quetzalcoatlus

Unrepentant.
Carnivore.
Largest of all
flying things.
How the timid
must have trembled
in the shadow
of your wings.

CRETACEOUS PERIOD
144 – 65 million years ago

Tyrannosaurus rex

Rest in peace,
Old Meat-Eater.
No list would
be complete
without you.
Tyrant! King!
You thought
(if you could think)
you'd live forever.
The great *T. rex*
would never die!

But even kings
are vanquished
when stars fall
from the sky.

CRETACEOUS PERIOD
144 – 65 million years ago

Titanoboa and *Carbonemys*

The largest snake
that's lived on Earth,
you weighed a ton
(a three-foot girth),
your length not short
of marvelous.

And then there is *Carbonemys,*
with whom you shared a habitat.

It frightens me to think of that.

PALEOGENE PERIOD

65 – 24 million years ago

Megalodon

We think of you as heartless.
We are wrong:
Of hearts, you had hundreds.
        Sharp!
And seven inches long.

Smilodon

No compassion.
No tolerance.
No mercy.
No pity.
And definitely no
"Here, kitty, kitty, kitty."

Megatherium

Rhymes with *delirium*—
appropriate
it seems
since you
and all those like you
are the stuff of
mega-dreams.

NEOGENE PERIOD
24 – 1.8 million years ago

Mammuthus

If you're like your modern cousin,
your memory is good.
What then, shaggy one,
would you remember
if you could?
White moonlight
shining on the herd?
The hard and driving rain?
Or the scent of danger
on the frozen plain?

A NOTE FROM THE AUTHOR

One of the challenges of writing a book like this is that new discoveries are made every day. At the time of publication, *Quetzalcoatlus* is considered to be the largest flying animal that has ever lived. But who knows? Tomorrow the fossil of a new, even larger flying reptile might be uncovered. One day you're the biggest; the next, you're not.

Our information about these animals is constantly evolving, but one thing that will always be true is that they lived a long, long time ago. Most scientists believe that Earth is about 4.5 billion years old. For most of that time, life on our planet was pretty simple. But in a geologic era called the Precambrian, things began to get interesting, and by the next period, the Cambrian, life exploded.

In the Past begins there, in the Cambrian, about 540 million years ago, and ends in the Quaternary, which began about 1.8 million years ago. It includes poems about animals from each of the periods in between. Think of those geologic periods as a staircase, with each one a step closer to modern times. You might be surprised to find that the Quaternary hasn't ended yet. In other words, humans share a geologic period with woolly mammoths and cave bears.

All but one of the animals pictured in the book are extinct. I wonder if you can guess which one it is.

NOTES ON THE ANIMALS:
THE FACTS THAT INSPIRED THE POEMS

CAMBRIAN PERIOD (544–505 million years ago)

Trilobite (TRY-luh-bite): More than fifteen thousand different species of trilobites have been identified, and more are being discovered every year. But what's a clock doing in a poem about the trilobite? Earth's crust is made of many layers, and the deeper you dig, the older the layer. Scientists think of this system of layers as a geologic clock. What's more, trilobites are the ancestors of that modern-day pest, the tick.

ORDOVICIAN PERIOD (505–438 million years ago)

Astraspis **(as-TRAS-pis):** Whenever we think of prehistoric animals, our imagination almost always goes to the great dinosaurs of the Mesozoic: *Apatosaurus, Stegosaurus, T. rex.* But it's important to remember that not all life comes in big packages. *Astraspis,* for example, which appeared hundreds of millions of years before the dinosaurs, was tiny. Like a tadpole.

SILURIAN PERIOD (438–410 million years ago)

Eurypterus **(yoo-RIP-ter-us):** *Eurypterus* had five pairs of leg-like appendages. The first and smallest pair was used for tearing its food apart, the next three for capturing its prey and for walking along the sea floor, and the last for swimming. Some paleontologists believe that while *Eurypterus* lived most of its life in the water, it also spent some time on land. I don't think I'd enjoy a family reunion with *Eurypterus.* Scorpions would be at the table. Spiders, too!

DEVONIAN PERIOD (410–360 million years ago)

Dunkleosteus **(dunk-lee-OH-stee-us):** At the time it lived, *Dunkleosteus* was at the top of the food chain. It was huge! Twenty to thirty feet long! And with an appetite to match, chomping its razor-sharp jaws (no teeth!) down on anything in the water that was foolish enough to get close. The fossil record tells us that Big D.'s fossils are often associated with the vomited, partly digested remains of its lunch. Ew!

CARBONIFEROUS PERIOD (360–286 million years ago)

Meganeura **(meg-uh-NYER-uh):** This insect had a wingspan of nearly thirty inches! *Meganeura* wasn't actually a dragonfly. It belonged to a different order from our modern-day garden dwellers.

Arthropleura **(ar-throh-PLER-uh):** Paleontologists believe that one of the reasons creatures like *Meganeura* and *Arthropleura* grew so large was the high percentage of oxygen in the atmosphere during the period in which they lived, a whopping 35 percent! Compare that to today's 21 percent. You should be happy about that decrease. Imagine how big your baby brother would be now if he lived three hundred million years ago.

PERMIAN PERIOD (286–248 million years ago)

Dimetrodon **(dye-MET-ruh-don):** *Dimetrodon* was no slouch in the size department—as much as eleven feet long and five hundred pounds. But looks can be deceiving. It was not a dinosaur. In fact, it lived about fifty million years before the first dinosaurs appeared. Some paleontologists believe that *Dimetrodon*'s sail soaked up the sun during the daytime to help keep it warm at night. Kind of like the first solar panel.

TRIASSIC PERIOD (248–208 million years ago)

Eoraptor (EE-oh-RAP-ter): This beastie is one of the earliest dinosaurs and great-great-grandpa to some of the giants that appeared later. Funny, when you realize that it was only about three feet tall, the size of a turkey. *Eoraptor* might have been pint-size, but it was also a serious carnivore with dozens of very sharp teeth. That's one scary Thanksgiving dinner!

JURASSIC PERIOD (208–144 million years ago)

Dilophosaurus (dye-LOH-fuh-SAW-rus): *Dilophosaurus* was made famous by the movie *Jurassic Park*. Maybe because it had the original Mohawk! Unfortunately, the moviemakers didn't get it right. *Dilophosaurus* didn't spit poison the way it did in the flick, it wasn't the size of your neighbor's dog (it was bigger—much, much bigger), and it didn't have that weird neck thing. Oh, well. I still like the movie. But I wonder if *Dilophosaurus* would have.

Stegosaurus (STEG-uh-SAW-rus): Poor *Stegosaurus*. Paleontologists tell us it was kind of a dummy. But it must have been doing something right. It was on the planet about fifteen million years.

Apatosaurus (uh-PAT-uh-SAW-rus): In 1877, a paleontologist named Othniel Marsh discovered the bones of a new species of dinosaur. He named it *Apatosaurus*. Later, he discovered some bones of what he thought was a *different* dinosaur. He named it *Brontosaurus*. But later, scientists said those bones were only the remains of a more mature *Apatosaurus*. So, according to them, *Brontosaurus* never existed. In other words, there never was a "thunder lizard"! That's kind of sad. But there is hope for *Brontosaurus* yet. In April 2015, scientists in Europe said they had evidence that *Brontosaurus* should be reinstated. That's kind of happy.

Brachytrachelopan (BRAK-ee-TRAK-el-OH-pan): *Brachytrachelopan* is a kind of dinosaur called a sauropod, and sauropods—like *Brachiosaurus* and *Apatosaurus*—are supposed to have those long necks and tiny heads. Tiny brains, too, unfortunately. (Sorry, *Apatosaurus,* but you weren't exactly a genius.) Then along comes *Brachytrachelopan,* with its short neck and big head, breaking all the rules of what sauropods are supposed to look like. Let's hear it for the weirdos!

CRETACEOUS PERIOD (144–65 million years ago)

Yutyrannus (yoo-tye-RAN-us): You can probably tell by looking at this oddball's name that it's a relative of *T. rex*. It's not fair to call it an oddball, I guess, but it was covered with small, fuzzy feathers, something like a three-thousand-pound, very hungry chicken. *Yutyrannus* was discovered in China in 2012 and is the largest feathered dinosaur found to date.

Quetzalcoatlus (KET-zuhl-koh-AHT-lus): There's a lot of controversy about *Quetzalcoatlus*. Here's why: recent research on Ketzie, as I like to call it, suggests that it may not have flown at all. Instead, some scientists believe that it stalked its prey on the ground, walking upright like some kind of freaky Big Bird with leather wings, a much sharper beak, and a much worse temper. *Quetzalcoatlus* is named for the ancient Aztec god Quetzalcoatl. The name means "feathered serpent."

Tyrannosaurus rex (tye-RAN-uh-SAW-rus reks): *Tyrannosaurus* and all the non-avian (non-birdlike) dinosaurs were wiped out sixty-five million years ago in a great extinction that some paleontologists believe was caused by an asteroid hitting Earth. That extinction marked the end of the Age of Dinosaurs.

PALEOGENE PERIOD (65 – 24 million years ago)

Titanoboa (tye-TAN-oh-BOH-uh) and **Carbonemys (kar-bun-EE-mis):** Every time I read about *Titanoboa*, its buddy *Carbonemys*, a snapping turtle the size of a Volkswagen Beetle, pops up. Even paleontologists, it seems, like to imagine what might have happened when these two monsters, both equipped with powerful jaws, met.

NEOGENE PERIOD (24 – 1.8 million years ago)

Megalodon (MEG-uh-luh-don): *Megalodon* is the biggest marine predator that ever lived. It weighed in at somewhere around one hundred tons. The average great white shark, in comparison, tips the scale at just three tons. What a shrimp! At any given time, *Megalodon* had a mouthful of more than two hundred heart-shaped teeth that could be up to seven inches long. But it was not exactly a valentine.

Smilodon (SMY-luh-don): What a disappointment to learn that the saber-toothed tiger is not a tiger at all and should be called instead a saber-toothed cat. *Smilodon* was nearly as big as a lion and had a couple of serrated canine teeth that could be as long as seven inches. Hard to believe that this kitty cat is related to the one that sits on your lap and purrs. Be happy you don't have to empty its litter box.

Megatherium (meg–uh-THEER-ee-um): The giant sloth is just one example of the megafauna (big animals) that lived during the Pleistocene Epoch, or Ice Age. *Megatherium* stood twelve feet tall on its hind legs. But it wasn't alone. It shared the planet with other giants: giant bears, giant camels, giant elks, even giant beavers.

QUATERNARY PERIOD (1.8 million years ago – present)

Mammuthus (MAM-uh-thus): Elephants really do have good memories. Their ancestors the woolly mammoths died out only ten thousand years ago. In geologic time, that's hardly the blink of an elephant's eye.

To Sebastian Chamberlain,
who told me I "had to" write
this book.
D. E.

For Oscar and Ripley
M. T.

First edition 2018

Library of Congress Catalog Card Number pending
ISBN 978-0-7636-6073-4

17 18 19 20 21 22 CCP 10 9 8 7 6 5 4 3 2 1

Printed in Shenzhen, Guangdong, China

This book was typeset in Columbus.
The illustrations were done in mixed media.

Candlewick Press
99 Dover Street
Somerville, Massachusetts 02144

visit us at www.candlewick.com